The Ma

by

Hazel Townson

Illustrated by Vicki Cosens

Dedication

For the staff and pupils of Hollins Grundy Primary School, Bury, who produced such good creative writing.

First published July 01 in Great Britain by

Educational Printing Services Ltd.
Albion Mill, Water Street, Great Harwood, Blackburn BB6 7QR
Telephone (01254) 882080   Fax (01254) 882010
e-mail:enquiries@eprint.co.uk   web site:www.eprint.co.uk

ISBN 1-900818-12-4

Contents

The Magic Pen . . .

Stories are magic!

. . . But you don't need to be a magician to write one.

Just pick up your pen.

Your pen is magic . . .

It is packed with stories.

All it needs is a few little pushes from you.

First Push

Your pen needs a notebook

... *Find one today!*

Carry the notebook everywhere you go so that whenever you come across an idea for a story you can jot it down.

You never know when that might be.

Inspiration can strike at any moment.

If you don't jot your idea down it will be quickly forgotten and lost forever.

Second Push

Your notebook needs an idea.

Use your eyes . . .
Look around the room . . .
What do you see . . .

Perhaps a plant that may grow and grow until it takes over the room, the house, the town . . .

Maybe you can see nothing more exciting
than a coat on a hanger . . .

but suppose that coat climbed off the
hanger and walked across the room

. . . becoming a haunted coat?

Or what about
that cupboard
. . . could it have
a secret drawer?

and wonderful things can happen on

. . . flying carpets!

If the room gives you no ideas, look through the window. You may see two birds on a branch . . .

Are they

chatting?

Quarrelling?

Hatching a plot?

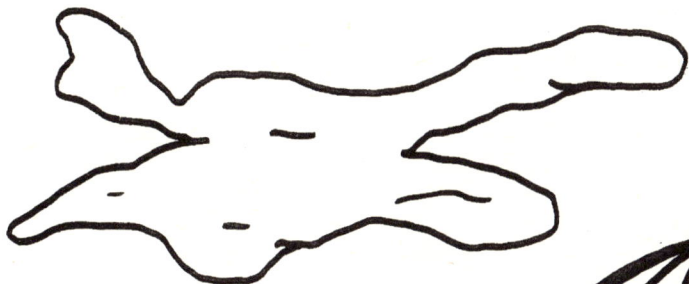

Or you may see a
strangely dressed
passer-by;
a stalking cat;
a weird cloud shape
that might turn
out to be
something from
outer space.

If your note book is still empty, take it outside. Look at your surroundings.

You may be inspired by:
   . . . a garden,
   . . . a dark alley,
   . . . a mysterious looking house

or even . . .
an unusual door knocker!

If there are people around what are they doing?

**Hurrying? Dawdling? Meeting?
Parting? Arguing?**

What sort of lives do you imagine they lead?

Could they have secrets?

Browse among shop windows.

Toy shops and **antique shops** especially will be full of interesting or unusual things.

And what about a shop selling **magic tricks . . .**

. . . or one that **hires out costumes?**

Visit an art gallery . . . **One of the pictures may give you an idea for a story.**

That happened once to me.

I looked at a picture of a country lane, then I looked again, and the second time I saw a tiny figure in the distance which I had not noticed before.

So then I thought,

'Suppose the figure was not always there, but came and went up and down the lane?'

The result was a **Ghost Story** about a haunted picture.

*Spend some time in
a museum . . .*

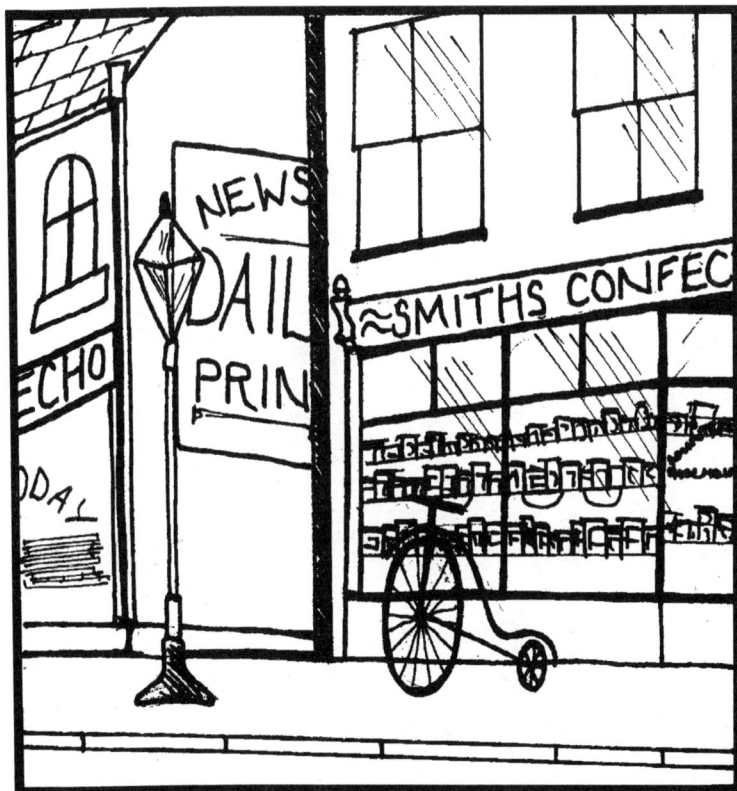

Museums these days
are not boring places but are
imaginatively designed to
bring the past to life.

Many of them have reconstructions of rooms in houses from the past, or even whole streets.

Some museums deal especially with costume or toys, science or transport.

Decide what interests you and seek it out.

Other places to visit might include a
**fairground, park, zoo, railway station,
market . . .**

. . . any place where people and objects
may be found to **suggest a story.**

Look at the children's news programme on BBC television at 5.00 p.m. on weekdays.

Writers borrow lots of ideas from the news. Actual events can be changed a little to make similar stories.

For instance:

. . . there was once a news item about some boys who found an old wardrobe in an empty house and chopped it up to put the pieces on their bonfire. When they were chopping it up they found a dirty old newspaper parcel behind a sliding panel. Inside the parcel there was *£10,000 in notes!*

Think of the possibilities!

Did the money belong to an old lady who had lost her memory and forgotten where she put the notes?

or

was the money hidden
by bank robbers who
were then caught and
unable to collect it?

Maybe it was a
kidnap ransom
. . . meant to be
collected later?

Perhaps the money was counterfeit,

produced on a machine hidden in the cellar?

Besides using your eyes . . .
use your ears.

Notice scraps of conversation as you walk past people or sit near to them on the bus or train.

No need to listen in rudely to a whole conversation.

Just notice and remember little phrases you can't help overhearing. I once heard a woman telling her friend that her son had come home *'covered from head to foot in blue dye'*.

I thought this would make an unusual idea for a story and used it in a book called **'Blue Magic'** in which the heroine is dyed blue.

Another time a train passenger explained that her son *'wouldn't go anywhere without his sticking plasters'.*

This gave me an idea for a story called **'Disaster Bag'**

In 'Disaster Bag', the boy hero of the book, is so worried about the state of the world and all its dangers that he carries around with him a disaster bag filled with everything he might need in a crisis.

Unfortunately, when he's not looking, a hunted terrorist slips a bomb into the bag!

Listen to the radio now and then as a change from looking at television or videos.

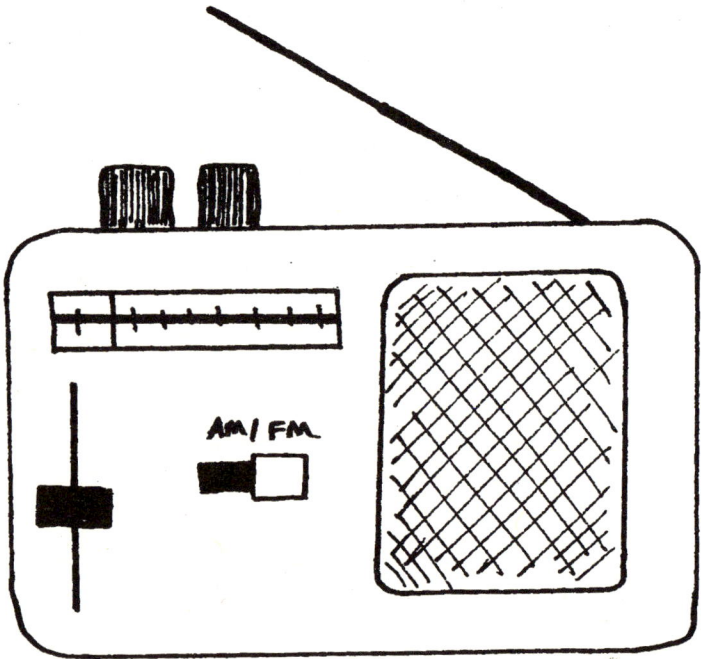

Radio will make you use your *imagination* because you will have to picture things for yourself.

There are often stories, plays and other items suitable for children on Radio 5.

Think back to your own early days . . .
Did something **strange** or **special** or
exciting happen to you then?

If you didn't have any really adventurous
moments you could always embroider the
things that did happen to make them
seem more interesting.

For instance . . . if you fell over in the paddling pool you could pretend the water was much deeper than it actually was

and that you then had an
Under-Water Adventure!

Ask other people for their memories, too.

Your parents, grandparents, other relatives, friends or neighbours

might be able to tell you some interesting things that happened to them.

When you have found your idea, scribble it down in your notebook in any old way.

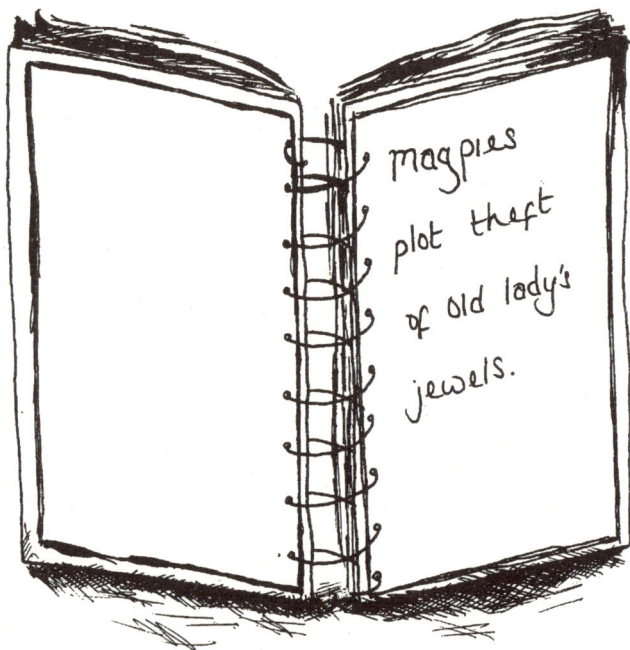

magpies
plot theft
of old lady's
jewels.

DO THIS AT ONCE!

Do not wait or the idea will vanish.

Just a few words will do at first . . .
enough to remind you of your thoughts.

Third
Push

Your idea needs a shape!

How do you shape a story?

You need a **good, exciting beginning,** so that the reader is immediately gripped by your story and wants to read on.

Start with a piece of action rather than a long description.

Once you have the reader's interest you must hold on to it by keeping up the excitement all the time. Let one adventure lead to another. ***Don't allow boring bits to interrupt your story.***

If the boring bits do find a way in, then cross them out again, even if you think you have written them well. **The story comes first.**

Build your story up to a climax by making the reader wonder what on earth is going to happen next and . . .

keep a big surprise for the end!

The best kind of story is one which the reader does not want to put down until he or she has finished it . . .

***and finds out
what finally happens!***

Never begin with the title!

If you do, you will be stuck with it although you may want to change the direction of your story once you get under way.

The title should be the last thing you write, choosing it from an exciting bit of the story to tempt the reader.

Some of my titles have been . . .

'The Shrieking Face',
'The Great Ice-Cream Crime'
and
'The Vanishing Gran'.

Don't worry yet about the length of your story.

Write it the way it feels best.

If it is too long you can always cut it down later. If you think it is too short, the odds are that you will spoil it if you add **'padding'** for no other reason than to make it longer.

Don't worry about who is going to read your story . . .

A good story should be readable by anyone up to the age of one hundred.

Don't believe that you have to put lots of fancy words and phrases into your story in order to be a real author.

> "The headgear worn by the gentleman was of a dark colour."

The simplest words are usually the best!

> "The man's hat was black."

Write clearly and do not make your sentences too complicated.

The reader should not have to go back and read bits over again in order to make sense of them. If you are using dialogue, read those bits out loud to see if they sound right.

Fourth
Push

Your story shape needs characters.

These should be as real as possible.

It is best not to use people you have met or they may be very upset when they find out.

What you can do is take little bits of various people you know and mix those bits together . . .

to make a new character.

Once you have decided what each of your characters looks like you should be able to describe them well enough for the reader to picture them.

You need to decide on their behaviour, too.

How would a character react to certain situations?

Would he:

speak softly or loudly,
bully younger children,
answer adults cheekily,
react bravely or cowardly in a crisis?

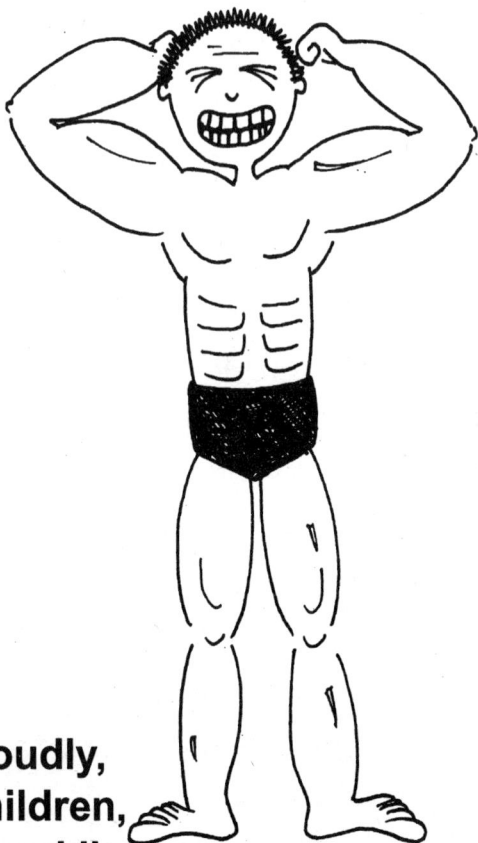

Notice the way people around you behave.

Ask yourself which ones annoy you, and why?

Is it because they are greedy, boastful, mean, aggressive?

Which kinds of people are more likely to help you if you are in trouble?

Notice what it is that makes popular people popular.

Listen to the way people speak, for your characters must sound real.

Hi Dad!

For instance,
if a child meets
his father in the
street he will be more
likely to say
'Hi, dad!' than
'Good day father!'

If you get the speech right your characters will come to life much more convincingly. Read the dialogue aloud, and if possible get someone else to listen and give their opinion.

Take care with the characters' names! These are very important and a wrong-sounding name can spoil your characters.

If you are stuck for names scan the telephone directory for surnames, then search in your local library for books of boys' and girls' first names. Don't use similar names for several characters in the same story or the reader will become confused.

Even names that don't sound alike but look alike on the page may create confusion.

You don't want your reader to have to search back several pages to find out who did what.

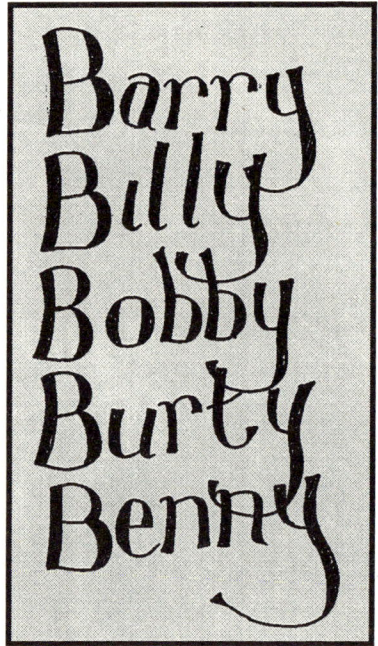

Barry
Billy
Bobby
Burty
Benny

Remember that if your character behaves in one way at the beginning of the book he must go on behaving in the same way unless you make something happen to change him.

. . . A sweet and generous heroine should not suddenly turn vicious and nasty unless you show a very good reason for it.

If you want to write about a particular profession or job, such as a **sailor, policeman, fireman,** etc . . . , it is both fun and good sense to find out more about the subject first.

Ask someone who has first-hand experience or search for information on the internet or in books.

The children's librarian in your local library will always help you to find any information you need . . . it is part of her job.

People may advise you to write only about things you know well, but if all authors did this we should have a very dull set of books on our shelves.

Don't be afraid to use your imagination!

Lewis Carroll had never been down a rabbit hole and Tolkien had never met a Hobbit.

Above all, **you should enjoy what you write.**

You are sharing your characters' adventures without risking your own life and limb.

Fifth
Push

Your story may be finished now . . .

But it needs REVISING!

You will probably think this is the boring bit. Once you have written **'The End'** you may not want to think about your story again.

Perhaps you are tired of it or eager to show it to someone and earn a bit of praise.

Or maybe you are keen to start off on the next idea. But you do need to **improve on the first draft** of the story.

If you read it through again you will find there are better words you could have used here and there. (Something more imaginative than **'got'** or **'big'** or **'nice'** for instance).

Perhaps you have repeated a word several times . . . See if you can replace some of the repeats with alternatives. If you have described something more than once cut out all but the best description.

Read your plot through carefully to make sure there are no mistakes of timing. If your hero is on his way home to tea at the beginning of chapter one, yet is eating his breakfast within half an hour, there is something wrong somewhere.

Similarly, if he is at school in Brighton on Monday morning, he is unlikely to be on an elephant safari in Timbuctoo on Monday afternoon!

. . . and have you made sure there are elephants in Timbuctoo?

Be careful to tie up all the loose ends of your plot by the close of the story.

If the heroine's cat disappears the reader will want to know whether it turns up again. The most satisfactory way to tie up loose ends is to *let the hero or heroine win through after many difficulties . . .*

and *make sure the villain gets his come-uppance,* even if he has been doing well for himself right through the story.

You need the reader's approval of the way things have turned out.

In fact, the very last bit of your story should make the reader sigh with satisfaction and say,

'I really enjoyed that!'

Then he or she will be eager to read the next story that flows from your **'Magic Pen'**.

Story Ideas

❑ **Here are 10 story ideas for you to try.**

❑ **Look at all the different possibilities in each idea.**

❑ **Choose the story-line you like best**

❑ **. . . and then work out what will happen.**

Two children find a wallet full of money. The owner's name and address is inside. One child wants to return the wallet to that address but the other wants to keep it.

Who wins the argument?
. . . and what happens then?

Three children are on their way to a party at a cliff-top house. Each is carrying a present. One child slips and his present falls over the cliff edge. The children climb down to the beach to look for the present and make an exciting discovery.

What could this be?

... **Signs of a shipwreck?**
... **Valuable flotsam?**
... **Weird footprints in the sand?**
... **A cave in which they explore and become trapped?**

Twins (a boy and a girl) are staying with their Gran whilst their mother is in hospital. Gran's house stands alone at the edge of a wood with no near neighbours. One day Gran climbs a ladder into the attic to fetch some old photographs. She slips, bangs her head and lies unconscious on the attic floor.

Do the twins know what to do? If they climb up into the attic to help, perhaps the ladder falls and they are all trapped up there. Or maybe Gran is not badly hurt, but her fall has revealed some treasured possession she didn't know was there. If Gran is badly hurt, perhaps she will have to go to hospital, so then what will become of the twins?

Jack and Gary are walking home from school together when they see a man climbing in through a back window of Gary's house. They ring the police on Jack's mobile but are not believed because there have been lots of hoax calls from local children and the police think this is another hoax. So the boys decide to lay a trap for the burglar themselves.

How do they do this? . . . and does their plan succeed? Maybe this wasn't a burglar after all but a kind passer-by helping Gary's mum who has lost her key?

Joanne wants to buy her mother a Christmas present but she has no money. She decides to steal a brooch from a department store but is spotted by a store detective who gives chase. She runs out of the store in a panic. Is she caught, or does she manage to escape? If she escapes, does she feel guilty and decide to return the brooch? Maybe she just throws it away! Or does she still give it as a present?

Do you want the reader to feel sorry for Joanne or to disapprove of what she has done?

On a class outing to a bird sanctuary Josh and Bobby are bored and wander off by themselves. They see two men trying to snare some of the rarest birds. The boys run off to report it, but the men have seen them and give chase.

Do they catch up with the boys and threaten or possibly kidnap them? Or could a flock of birds come to the boys' aid by attacking the villains?

Gemma hears weird noises in the middle of the night. She gets out of bed, looks through her window and sees a strange blue light hovering over the lawn.

What could it be? A ghost? A space-ship? Someone trying to scare the family away because they want to live in the house? A figure with a lantern, searching for something?

Darren has a row with his dad and decides to run away.

He could take a bus to the village where his Gran lives and ask her to look after him. Or he could hide in the empty house at the end of the road. He could even hitch a lift to the city and try his luck there . . . Whichever choice he makes there are bound to be dire consequences.

The old lady who just moved next door to Jan seems rather weird. She wears strange black clothes. She talks to herself and to her huge black cat. She wanders about in the middle of the night and gathers plants and berries from the hedgerows.

When some of the villagers begin a cruel witch-hunt, will Jan make friends and come to the old lady's rescue? If she does try to help, will she find herself in danger, either from the 'witch' or from the angry villagers who resent her interference?

Mark has been invited to stay at his new friend Joel's house for the weekend. Mark is nervous; he doesn't make friends easily and is anxious to give a good impression. It's a large old house with a history and Mark finds it rather gloomy.

In his bedroom there is a huge mirror in a carved wooden frame. As he is unpacking on the first night he looks into the mirror and sees a dark figure standing behind him. When he turns there is no-one there.

Was it a ghost, or Joel playing a trick? Could there be someone living secretly in the house who had just looked in through the open door? Maybe it was a servant, detailed to keep an eye on him. Or perhaps it was nothing more than his own imagination which might well ruin his weekend and the whole new friendship.

<u>Remember!</u>

First Push!
   Your Pen Needs a Notebook

Second Push!
   Your Notebook Needs an Idea

Third Push!
   Your Idea Needs a Shape

Fourth Push!
   Your Story Shape Needs Characters

Fifth Push!
   Your Story May be Finished . . . but it Needs Revising

Good Luck!